I don't know what I'm doing
I think it's important that
If I give you this
And you accept it
That you understand
I have no idea what I'm doing
But I suppose
None of us do
Not at first
(What will I do?)
Not really in the middle
(what am I doing?)
Even at the end
(what have I done)

Do we ever know what we do?

If you don't know what you're doing either
I've written this
For us

A Dedication

Copyright © 2020 by Justin El

All rights reserved. This book or any portion thereof may not be reproduced or used in any manner whatsoever without the express written permission of the publisher except for the use of brief quotations in a book review.

Printed in the United States of America.

Print ISBN 978-1-952987-15-1
eBook ISBN 978-1-952987-16-8

JANUS

A POETRY COLLECTION

JUSTIN EL

ACT I, PART I

Cleave /klēv/
[verb]
To become very strongly involved with or emotionally attached to (someone)

The clasp of hands
The little death
There are few things
More glorious than this

Shoot Your Shot

I fumble
Tripping on this red rug
In my mouth
Spilling compliments
Like children's crayons
All over your desk
I seem
Inexperienced
Overeager
Clumsy attempts
To tell you
Hello
I think you're cool
One day I'll learn
I'll say less

By Design

Anatomy is strange
My eyes look at you
But my heart sees you
My hands touch you
But my ears feel you
Who wired our bodies
So perfectly?

First Draft

I'm a writer, not a lover.
I will treat us like a book
No.
Revise.
Start.
Again.
I'm a writer, not a lover.
I would treat us like a manuscript
And take my time in our creation
I will obsess over you
Running fingers through the pages of our history
Trying to understand the meaning
in the spaces
between your words
I am fluent in the language of things left unsaid
When dawn creeps
warm fingers into the room
and discovers
us
in bed

My face will be buried between covers
Excavating your secrets
There is nothing like the smell of you
When I caress your spine
Are the ridges a code?
A haiku in Braille
I have more secrets
Than I think you can see, love
Seek them out with care
I am a writer, not a lover
Ours will be a saga
This is our draft
Let us revise it
Together

Geography

I love the fault lines in your earth
The shifts on the land
Of eyes, cheeks and lips
That form your smile
Your laughter is merry chaos
From the start of your roots
To the tips of your branches
Thank you for being
The stars burn brighter
With our worlds aligned

Night Lessons

My body remembers
The cold kiss of moonlight
We shined like stars
In the space
Between breaths and covers
The stellar death
Our supernova
Our universe shook
And fell silent

Every morning
The sunlight
Revealed the golden valleys of our skin
You traced your finger in slow, dizzying circles
Racing a comet across my chest
I'd set my teeth against your shoulder
To make sure you were real

I carry our cosmos on my skin
Tattoo galactic
A milky way memory
Courses through my cells
At night
When all is still
You will be the star I wish upon

Four Twenty

I hear the striking of a match
When our fingers touch
You set my soul afire

If I could bury my face
In the nap of your neck
And breathe in
Your essence
I'd never exhale

Crescendo

You lay your back against my chest
Arms a shawl around my shoulders
My fingers play your ribs
Like a harp
And the sound you make
Is sweeter than any orchestra
Sing for me

The Prophet & The Sailor

That night,
We lay in a sea of sheets and pillows
As the wind from our breaths soothed the sweat from our brows
I'd dreamed of you, she told me
Hair cascading over eyes the color of ancient oaks
Filled with promise and a certainty
That seemed to belong to someone older
I called her a prophet
And laid my hands on her altar
Whispering hymns with a lover's tongue
Until the choir cried out
And the storm abated
I don't know what tides brought me
Rudderless, coasting through my odyssey
To the beacon of your siren's call
But at least here, dear Calypso
On this island of limbs entwined
like rope to a mast
We can weather our storms together
If just for tonight

Beanstalk

The trick with surrounding yourself
With people
That you consider giants
Is that you must
Accept the truth
When they say
They see you
As tall as them

Love, Correctly

There is a difference between
Loving someone
Like you'd love a god
and
Loving someone
Because they make you feel
Godly
One melts your wings
One helps you fly

There is a difference between
Needing them
Like
You need air
and
Air tasting sweeter
In their presence
One leaves you breathless
One helps you breathe deeper

Pedestals are the perfect places to hang fools from
You are not a mountain to be conquered
A tower to be surpassed
But an ocean
To be discovered slowly
Tentatively
How could I ever know your depths
If I place you out of reach?

ACT I, PART II

Cleave /klēv/
[verb]
To split or sever (something), especially along a natural line or grain

The parting of ways
The hum of a tear
Before floodgates open
There are few things
More memorable

Itadakimasu

Let us break bread
Break ourselves
Open
Made vulnerable
Buttered smiles
Tears older than wine
They grow richer with age
Let us break fast
Share shards
of stories
Broken hearts
Promises unkept
In laying out our pieces
We make our holes
Whole, again
Let us
break

Explorer

I've lost myself on the forest of your hair
The valley of your smile
And stars in your eyes
I map, and chart
this world
 I traverse
Because one day
This land
May be a stranger to me

Intermission

Often
I stand in your doorways
And wonder
How many stories have started
And ended
In these thresholds
I want to
Bookmark here
And come back
When I'm braver
And ready
For the next chapter
I don't like endings
Beginnings make me anxious
Why can't we live
In the story
When the characters
Already know each other
When the villain
Doesn't exist
And the world is safe
Every day
Nothing closed
All is open
For all to see
Why can't we live
In the threshold?

Origami

Speak plainly
I've bloodied my hands on paper cuts
Unfolding the words you say

The Breakup

You kept the number
Treating it like a flame
Close enough for warmth
But never to touch
Lest you burn again

But it felt
So good
Tracing those digits
With your fingers

...In the Sea

The ocean swelled in their eyes as the child said
Today I lost a friend
The fisherman smiled
I have seen and lost
The most wondrous catch
But I cannot weep
They were never mine
To begin with
Perhaps tomorrow
I will find another

Arson

It will burn
This change
The tearing apart
From friends
From habits
From the life
You once were
It will burn
But not
Half as much
As the pain
Of staying the same

Advice for Meeting Exes

Never ask
If they've given their heart
To another
Especially if you haven't
Found yours since they
Lost it

Cardio

I don't care
How fast you run
Or how far you go
You'll soon tire
You'll soon turn
And have to
Face
Me

Sincerely,
The Heart

Gardening

Cry
Because seeds need water
And your soul wants to grow

Precious Memory

Sometimes, our moments burn
Hot coals in the furnace of my mind
I think
If I squeeze hard enough
I can remember them
For the diamonds they should have been

A Conversation

I wrote poems about you
That's sweet
No it wasn't
What was it then?
Recovery

That Damn Justin Timberlake Song

I would never lie to you
You said to me
But you could lie to yourself
And when you looked in my eyes
You looked into mirrors

Everest

Some of us
Treat love like mountain peaks
Admiring from afar
And ill equipped
For the task required to reach it

Etiquette

You cried over spilt milk
Shattering every china cup you've held since
Blaming that first time
Instead of learning
To prepare a better table

Scribbling in Marvin's Room

Whiskey tastes
Like words left unsaid
Some drink
Until their cups runneth over
Lips turn to levees
Bursting forth with all that we've held back
We create these accidents
And call this bravery

Tears from Alexander

The Macedonian wept
When the philosopher told him
Of infinite universes
Because he himself
Had not conquered one

I wept similarly
For in your smile
I could see every star
In your eyes
The promise of infinite possibilities
Now that you're gone
I fear I've lost them all

JUSTIN EL

Romantics are Hypocrites

I shouldn't
Give all of myself
And wonder why
I feel emptied
I shouldn't
Put you on a pedestal
And wonder why
you looked down upon me
I shouldn't
Carry your burdens on top of mine
And wonder why
My soul feels heavy
I shouldn't
But I do
And I wonder
Why

Vulcan's Apprentice

I drink deeply from a cup of memories
Until I pass out in drunken stupor
When I awaken
I wipe misplaced jigsaw puzzles from my lips
And try to gather your pieces
My hands are smeared with glue
And fragments of those I've tried to put together
My arms branded
From the nights I spent
Trying to forge old bonds
Into something new
Something that lasts
This time

I am a lover of damaged good
I tinker with broken things
Windup cars, yo-yos
And porcelain dolls with cracked faces
Deemed ugly for their exposure
Perhaps I love them
Because I see my gait in their halting steps
My tongue in the stammer of their words
My expression in eyes
That could speak before they were ever taught how
You are not broken
All the king's horses
And all the king's men
Do not see you as I do
I cannot heal you
Fix you
But I will try to do so
All the same

We Don't Talk Anymore

If asked
I will say that I don't think about you
Like I don't think to breathe
Like I don't think to blink
Like I don't think to sleep
I don't mean to
But it happens

Unfinished, Untitled

There is no library large enough
To hold the volumes
Your absence has written
But some stories are better left unread

Inhale

I used to breathe you
Now I breathe free
It's better this way

End It with Hope

I hope you've learned to grow.
I hope you've set your roots deep
And cling to your loved ones
Like vines creeping along the wall
Of a beautiful summer morning
I hope you stand tall in the sun, and dance in the rain
I hope you've learned to weather your storms
Bent, but unbroken.
Bearing your struggles like fruits
The weight is temporary
You will drop it when you're ready
And it'll be ever sweeter because of it
I hope you've learned to grow.

Medicine Is Necessary

The first time I skinned my knee
I was a child
All lanky limbs and wide eyes
Held together by innocence
And a belief that life
And all its intricate pattern
Was just simple fabric
Held together by the same thread
That quilted me

Playing in the hot grit
Of Benin sand
I'd tripped
My knee running roughshod
Over earth that would never
Be beaten into the civilized order
we called pavement
I soon found a patch of crimson glaring at me
over a flap of torn skin

My grandmother came to the sound of my cries
Alcohol burned
Like harsh words
And brought me peace
Like honest ones

I learned back then
That sometimes
What hurts us
Is precisely what we need
To not hurt again

For Angel

I remember your wake
So many came to see you
One last glimpse of the light
that drew us all together
Moths to a flame
Though when I drifted close enough
The reality of your passing burned my wings
And sent me crashing to my knees

I remember wondering
How could you think yourself so small
So unimportant
As if the weight of your absence
Would not throw so many out of orbit
As if your feet didn't step in time
With the heartbeat of everyone you met
I had to teach myself how to walk again
Since yours stopped beating

I have few pictures with you
Few moments to treasure and horde
Few ways to claim that we were kin
Few flags upon such to claim a moment as ours
Few, precious few
But we had moments, all the same

I almost joined you
One cold, rainy night
Dark liquor and darker words
Brought me to the edge of my strength
In that moment, I think
We understood each other
And maybe that thought
Is what saved me
I regret that it didn't save you

I carry you around, a tattoo on my soul
I fear that your image will fade with time
Until all that remains
Is your smile
And the rustle of laughter in the fall
But that smile
And that laugh
Are remnants of a better man
Than I could ever hope to be

I need you to know that I remember

Prosthetic

I just want to learn how to walk again
You don't realize how much you lean on someone
Until you've cut them off
And can't find your balance
Now every step
Feels like a lie
Your limbs aren't your own
And you're just hoping a doctor
Can re-attach
What you've lost

Daedalus Child

You know what falling feels like
You've taken leaps of faith
Flights of fancy
That Icarus wouldn't dare
You've spread your wings
And depended on their breath
To keep you up
To keep you safe
Now
Standing at the edge again
You look at the wings
You've stitched back together
And know better

Amputate
(The Gentrification Poem)

There is power in a name
Speak mine with care
My syllables are the rhythms of your tio
Both old and young
Salsero eternal
Dancing across your tongue
I taste like
Piraguas in the summer
Lips colored cherry
Coco mango rainbow
Cool as ice
Tito Puente's hands
Score the soundtrack of my heartbeat
I am revelry at the festival
Pride at the parade

There is power is a name
My voice is the rumble of dirtbikes
ATVs laughing down first avenue
On the first warm day of the year
Find my smile
In the glint of basketball trophies
At Jefferson Park
My eyes
Are the rainbows veiled

In the midst of the hydrant's spray
My Cotton Club suit? Adorned in Langston hues
Green as the ivy that rises like the sun
My energy sizzles like Dipset symphonies
Chopped cheese at Hajiis
The crack of the stickball bat
Dominoes forming constellations
In the universe of El Barrio

So when you subject my name
To the sloth of your tongue
And chop it down
Into letters that fit on a price tag
Understand what you do
My name rolls like a crescendo
Flowing waterfall
And in your ignorance you place levees
On the waters of a culture
Spanish Harlem
East Harlem
Two sides of a currency that cannot be minted
Except in the hearts of its people
Spa Ha?
Nah, b.
We're fine as we are.
There is power in a name

JANUS

Alchemists Create Closure

With a word they
Makes oceans of tears
And learns to rise
Above the tide

With a word they
Make lions of lambs
A pond of the storm
That they were never taught to sail

Our words have power
We put lead to paper
And give you gold

We transmute our pieces
Disparate and scattered
Amidst books and voices
Together, we can feel whole again

ACT II, PART I

Fast /fast/
[Adjective]
Moving or capable of moving at high speed

The quickened breath
The fleeting thought
The rush
The life

[M]y [T]rain [A]pproaches

An armored serpent
Makes its way through a maze
If it spoke
I wonder
If it would be as scared
Of the future
As I am

We tunnel our way through labrinths
Cells in the veins of our city
Every voyage a promise
Of adventure
Of a story
All aboard the silver behemoth
Next stop
Everywhere

Speed Dating

I once met someone who said
"I don't like talking on the phone,
it's too personal."
Later that night I wondered
If I'd ever really "met" them
And if they'd ever truly "met"
Anyone
At all

Muki-haiku

Remember your rights
Even if you have done wrong
For some roads go left

Life Imitates Life

It's funny how we live
Hard as rocks
Filled with fire
On a giant rock
Filled with fire
Spinning around
The greatest fire
We'll ever know

Rebel

Sometimes I jump
As high as I can
For no other reason
Than to defy physics
Telling myself
Though the world is built
To sit me down
When I try
I can rise
And rise
And rise

Howl

With the sun high
We move en masse
Sheep in the field
Of this slaughterhouse city
At night, we cast aside our wool
In your eyes, I see the wolf in me

ACT II, PART II

Fast /fast/
[Adjective]
To be hard to move; firmly or securely

The caged breath
The thoughts that linger
The wait
Still, life

JANUS

The Pokémon Poem

Evolution is
Scary to me because life
Has no B button.

A Mantra for Fortitude

My cup runneth over
With memories of mountains climbed
I will not let this hill
Make a drought of me

A Mantra for Patience

Be kind, friend
The world is sharp enough
Filled with jagged paths and hidden traps
You need not make an enemy
In the mirror as well

Distance

I waste
So much time
In worthless chases
Trying to catch up
To time I've lost
As if my legs
Will stretch time
Backwards
By running forwards
A treadmill
Would call that
Standing still
One day
I'll learn
To just enjoy
The run

Scope

I used to want
To write of ocean depths
And the grandeur of mountain peaks
Rolling verdant
Gilded by the morning lips of the Sun
But now I try
To find a drop of dew
Resting from the tip of a blade
Of grass on the mountain
Shimmering emerald
Warmed by a brilliance it knows but cannot explain
A stranger in a world
It was born in, and never left
I will find it
And tell you its story

Bleu Sand

You are like an hourglass
No matter where you turn
You always seemed to be running out of time
If I could shatter your cage
I'd bid you to sit
And run your fingers through the sand
Enjoy the present
Instead of wondering
How much you have left

Untitled

Here at least
There is peace
I discard myself
I am refuse
Flotsam and jetsam
Afloat and alone

Here at least
There is quiet
Shelter from the storm
From goals and from failures
Safe from others
Safe from myself

Here at least
There is rebirth
Time to renew
Time to remember
Time to try again
Here

Kindling

Wisdom comes to me at night
In my dreams it speaks to me
Mountains of it
When I wake, the glory vanishes into smoke
All I'm left with are sparks from the fire
Maybe that's the lesson
Sometimes I don't need to burn
Just glow
Enough to stay warm
In the long night

Northern Trees

Sneakers hang from lamp posts
Like so many strange fruit
The ghost of Billie Holiday
In a city that never sleeps

Salvation

There are those that are homeless
And those who have never known a home
It'll take a little more
Than small change
To help either of them

Untitled

We harp about our beginnings
For they are known.
They are fixed
It's our becoming
That terrifies us

More Gardening Tips

When I bring you roses
I leave the thorns on them
As a reminder
Removing someone's edges
Will not make them easier to love

Reflection

Does the sun seem sad to you?
I wonder if she knows
How many of us
Have grown from her smile
Maybe
The moon is her lover
Holding a mirror to her eyes
Maybe
On windy nights
You can hear their conversation
Oh my darling
Look how brightly you shine

A Haunting

At night, the ghosts of my regrets sit beside me
I used to hate them
Until I stopped
screaming
long enough
to hear what they were telling me.
You're still here.
At night, the ghosts of my regrets sit beside.
We smile upon old times.

A Square is a Square

Abstract art upsets me
The modern art
The layers of symbolism in painted squares
The hidden social commentary in the wreckage of an old car
What canvas can confuse me more
What sculpture can capture my attention
What can bring more tears to my eyes
Than life?
I write to give myself an anchor
Because life is the storm
That blows your expectations to ruin
And rains upon the seeds of your next hope
The world is abstract enough
I cannot find meaning in all I do
And I need something to make sense
So at least just tell me this picture of an orange
Is just a picture of a fucking orange

Vegvisir

I'd give my left my eye for wisdom
For the knowledge of knowing what will become of me
But I suppose fools learn to see
By rushing blindly
Wayward traveler
Your thoughts and memories
Perch upon your shoulders
Anchoring you firmly in the ocean of your life
Hold fast to who you are
Made up of so many edges and bends
Straight paths and crooked forks
Like runes of old
Embrace yourself
For as long as you hold onto you
You will not lose your way
In storms or fair weather

Pyromancy

Candles entice me
Full of fire
Quick to burn
Unable to grow
Without space to breathe
At night
I'll cup one in my hands
And whisper
You're just like me

Geology 101

Baby
When I tell you that you're beautiful
Don't tell me you look rough
Like that's a bad thing
Don't you know
That's where diamonds are born?

Thread Count

If your lover's bed
Was composed
Of musical notes
Instead of thread counts
Would you sing their tune
Every morning?

Guide

I never wanted
To walk these roads
Get lost in brambles
And lose my way
But since I have
I'll give you
What little advice I can

Tetris

We lay
On this bed
Legs like
Lincoln logs
One atop the other
A fort of
Thighs and calves
Laughter and sweat
Hands
Are Lego blocks
Gripped tight
Fitting perfectly
We fit into each other
Two S shapes
She sleeps, spoons
Sighs, sure she soon
Will tire of this
Maybe
This is all perfect
Maybe
This is doomed to fail
Maybe
This is Tetris
And we'll get in
Where we fit in
Until the next game

Necromancy

On summer nights
A cold breeze
Performs magic
Along my arm
Flesh rises
Like memories of
fallen lovers
And sometimes
The touch
Of my new lover
Lays them to rest

ACT III, PART I

Dust /dəst/
[Noun]
Fine, dry powder consisting of tiny particles of earth or waste matter lying on the ground or on surfaces or carried in the air

The sediment
Of sentiments
The grit
On pages in a library
Footprints in the sand
A reminder
Of what was

Janus

The Old Colossus

Colossus, where is your welcome?
You hold your torch in judgment
Could its light have caused you to forget
The brown of your skin
Or is the green you embrace
The only color
Worthy of your Liberty?

Ouroboros

You are a constant change
A growing
The shedding of who you were
For who you will be
It's frightening
I know
But never stop
Push forward
As if you're running
Lest the old you
Swallows you whole

A Train

I watched a drifter on the train
Shed his shoes like
a second skin
Toes grime covered
Nails like jagged rocks in a mine
No one wanted to be near him
And I don't think he cared
I think he just wanted
A brief respite
A moment to sit
In his truth
As ugly as it may seem
I think
I write
For the same reason

Residue

Just because
You aren't
The title
To my poems
Doesn't mean
I haven't written your name
Between the lines

Flotsam & Jetsam

Sailing through a sea
Of sunken friendships
Maybe
If you'd remembered that
These oars were made for two
We could've stayed afloat

Medical Advice

Memories are like wounds
The fingers of my mind
Keep picking at our scabs
My doctor
If I had one
Would tell me
That bleeding again
Won't heal the tear

Breakfast

Your smile
Was the golden brown
Of warm syrup
On Sunday pancakes
I told myself
I'd spend
My entire life
Being worthy of that smile
Maybe that's all we are
Just shades
Trying to find
A special smile
To be worthy of

Justin El

For Those That Burn Bridges

Some things
Are beyond
The greatest alchemy
To repair
And try as you might
You cannot build wood
From ashes

In Memory of Knighthood

Sitting in a corner
On the cheap side of the city
A silly boy
Slinging pebbles at the shadows
Of giants in my dreams
I learned of your legend
Sir William Thatcher
I know how you got your scars
Palms burned raw
From the effort of pulling constellations out of alignment
You taught me how to change my stars
If I knew nothing else about you that would be enough
The news of your passing was a lance
To an unarmored chest
Pain I was not prepared for
Never realizing how much you had given me
A squire with dreams of knighthood

When I am lost, I still follow my feet
And when they speak of my lady
I will tell them that she is not a target
But the arrow
When my arm struggles to hold the lance

And shadows taunt me saying
I have been weighed
I have been measured
And have been found wanting
I consider your battles
Jousting with those
Who would watch the world burn
I would spend a year in silence
To better understand your whispers
Amidst the rumbling of tournament horses
And the mad man's laugh
Saying
"It is not in me to withdraw. "
Nor I, Sir Thatcher.
Nor I.
But it happens

ACT III, PART II

Dust /dəst/
[Verb]
Remove the dust from the surface of (something) by wiping or brushing it

*The smell of dirt
After rain
The coming quake
Tremors in the sand
A foretelling
Of what will be*

Sobriety Chip

I almost had a drink today
But didn't
Deciding that
Dark words, darker thoughts
And darkest whiskey
Is a shade too black
To paint my
soul with
So if
you see me
Pour a glass
Of water
On my face
Maybe
I'm retracing my steps
To my Baptism
Just trying
To remember
My name
Just trying
To start again

But Did You Die?

I could tell you that
When you wake up
It won't hurt anymore
But I'd be lying
I could tell you that
When you wake up
You wouldn't remember them
But you know better
But I can tell you
That you'll wake up
And keep waking up
Even when it seems the world
Ended
The night before
And ain't that beautiful

When Nightmares Dream

If the ghosts of your mistakes
Could be haunted
It would be by the spectre
Of you
Walking away from them
Moving on
And never looking back

King of the Fall

Autumn gold dances with shadows
Upon a ballroom of your brown skin
You think of all the times you've been thriving, vibrant
And felt the beginnings of winter's chill
Of all the times you've become bare bones
Brown and feeble, swaying in the breeze
The leaves of your flesh crackling
Under the childlike feet of time
Change can be a killing
The small death of what was
To make way for what will be
But the glory of the fall lies in the rising
In the warm smile of the sun
Adorning the face of a misty morning
In the promise of the acorn
That seeks shelter in the soil
In the cold and the dark
To learn to grow
And emerge greater
Than it ever could imagine

end of

I realized that many people oscillate between hate and love.
I oscillate between hate and hope.

I hate the New Year.
I hate birthdays.
I hate anything that forces you to measure
your existence
your successes
your value
by units of time.

I hate hypocrisy
I hate failing
I hate failing people
More than I hate failing myself
And I really hate failing myself

I hate that being a writer makes me so damn introspective.
I hate that I'm empathetic.
I hate crying.
I hate being mad.
I hate feeling everything, all the time.

I hate the cold
I hate being cold
I hate how much it hurts to be cold
I hate how much it hurts to be cold

And I hate when people act like they don't feel the hurt
I hate that we froze
I hate that you refused to thaw

I hate lying
I hate feeling like I have to lie
I hate feeling like a liar
Even when I'm telling the truth

I hate a lot of things.
But I hope for a lot of things, too.

I hope I figure it out
I hope I make it work
And I hope it makes me happy
Whatever "it" is
If you write because you're sad, because you're breaking and need to heal.
I hope that one day you no longer need to write.

I hope to be able to forgive
I hope to be forgiven
I hope to be understood
To be at peace with my choices
If only for a moment

I hope I stop hating mistakes
Seeing them
Making them
I hope I hate less
And learn more

Janus

I hope I can stop hiding
From my friends
And myself
I hope I can be
Better, more
Whole, more
Me?
What does that even mean?
How can I be a fraction of something
When I don't even know what it means to be whole?

I hope I can meet a friend
We look each other in the eyes and say
I'm not
Depressed
Anxious
Suicidal
Or scared
And then walk away
Knowing neither of us
Were lying

I hope they know you love them.
I hope you know they love you.
And if they don't love you

I hope you know that, too

I hope you never confuse your dreams with your goals.
I hope you turn your goals into
plans, and your plans manifest into
actions,
and those
actions
into reality.
Fly in your dreams.
Cast spells and befriend dragons.
Live in Wakanda.
Date SZA.
Joking on the SZA part.
SZA is a human being. Don't deify human beings. I hope you stop doing that.

I hate resolutions
But if you have any
I hope you're resolute
In pursuing them
And if you slip
I hope you know
That's okay

Postscript, for Writers

Human beings
Are just stories
That never end

I know poets
That have never written
But their lives
Are the greatest stanzas
I've ever read

So write

Write like paper is water
In the middle of a storm
And each pen stroke
Is the only thing
Keeping you afloat

Justin El

www.ingramcontent.com/pod-product-compliance
Lightning Source LLC
Chambersburg PA
CBHW012106090526
44592CB00019B/2675